A
Journal of Love

From the Heart of a
Woman

Janete Carter

A Journal of Love from The Heart of a Woman

By Janete Carter

Cover design by Paula McDade

Edited by James Millington

Layout by Sabrena LeRoy

First Edition, 2017

Dedication

This book is dedicated to my master and the lover of my soul, Jesus. I am finally at a place in my life of complete contentment and I know that you are more than enough for me. If it's your will and desire to be my Boaz, so be it! Your love for me has been better than life.

To my children Janna, Joshua, Joy and Caleb. You guys are gifts sent down from heaven to remind me of God's love. I love being your mommy.

To those of you who believed in me and supported me to see this book to the end. Thank you and I love you most sincerely.

CONTENTS

I.   You Had Me at Hello.................................1

II.   Sugar and Spice, All Things Nice.......................4

III. Peaches and Cream, Strawberries and Chocolate.....7

IV.   Peek a Boo, do you still see me?.................10

V.   No Thing compares to you.........................14

VI.   Fifty Shades of Pink.................................18

VII. Eyes Closed Wide and Shut.......................22

VIII. Sticks and Stones "Words Left Unspoken"...................26

IX.   I Love You, I Could Eat You Up..................30

X.   There You Go & Went, You're Gone!...........................34

XI.   Will You Still Love Me in the Morning?.....................37

XII. Conclusion.................41

INTRODUCTION

I present you with this journal of poems and dainties true. They are words that are written, expressions of love from me to you. I hope you're entertained, captivated and adore, reading every word that follows and your left wanting more. If literature excites you, the English vernacular your delight. I'm constrained to fascinate you, you're hypnotized as I recite. Every word that is written, allow to gently roll off your tongue, these ardent notes of candor you will hear like a love song. So, yield to loves deep longing as it yearns to know your name. You'll be haunted by your desires, consumed by lust untamed. Your soul will cry for more, rythmatic groaning's that cannot be explained; a perpetual feast of pleasure, yet knowing no shame. You'll experience moments of laughter, maybe a tear will roll from your face. Most assuredly inordinate heat, exuding from that certain place. These words will transcend off of the pages and come alive. They'll enrapture, trap, and entangle your heart as they did mine. Enough said, shall we now begin. For you will see, hear, taste, and feel. All senses will experience my Journal of Love, I shall now reveal.

Acknowledgment

Pictures for 'A Journal of Love from the Heart of a Woman'

By, Janna Carter. Currently studying @ the School of the Art Institute of Chicago

You Had Me at Hello

Hello, simply hello, nothing more or less.
The first word you would utter the first time we met.
My ears will always remember the sound, pitch, and tone.
Where we were, the time and place, there we stood alone.
I'll forever remember, never forget the countenance of your face.
It was finished, you had won, did you know?
You had me at hello.

Chapter 1

The first time I ever heard your voice, it would be a sound I'd never forget. I would desperately wait with anticipation, hearing it over and over again. I would rehearse the very pitch in my inner ear, like a record played many times before. Comfort myself in remembrance as I silently listened - yes, your voice, did you know? I adore.

There would be a second-time fate would have me to meet you and that's the moment it hit me the hardest. You walked across the street - we were destined to meet. Coincidence or chance? I will never forget. Perhaps even, would it be safe to say that I was on my way to meeting you all of my life?

You bumped into me, and it was then, that brief encounter and exchange of words that would instantaneously pierce my very being to the core. Your voice was the gentlest of voices that I had ever heard, and that is what I most remember about that fateful day.

Did I fail to mention the very fact that you were easy on the eyes as well? I spend many days just thinking about you. This cycle is like a merry go round, spinning memories of you would play fervently inside my head. Can I tell you this? Right now, my heart and soul belong to you totally and completely.

I have not known you long - a month or maybe two, but what does that matter? I've fallen for you. Now that you're in my life, please make me your wife. I know I'm rushing this along really fast. Allow me to tell you this, it's your smile I can't resist, you're precisely all I had hoped for.

The very thought and notion of you has caused me to become unglued and my clothes slightly to become undone. Need I say more? For I have told you before - you had me at hello, you know? I'll leave you with this and it's sealed with a kiss, just one thing before you go. You should now and must know I'm yours and forever. I told you: "You Had Me at Hello"

Sugar and spice all things Nice
I'm inclined to believe that what I want and desperately need
is inconceivable to imagine because It's you.
You'll be the sugar on my tongue, the spice that's on my lip,
I'll ask you once and say it nice; come take a sip.
I'm sure you will agree, no need to beg on bended knee;
Whatever you ask of me or wish is my command.
Do unto me whatsoever you will.
drink up my love and let me fill your empty cup,

Chapter 2

The very first time I saw you, it would be years before I would ever meet you for the very first time in person. The second time would be similar to the first, but I was left with an impression and I might add, one that I would never forget. I could see that perhaps in some way, form or fashion that you were just a little lonely. It didn't show in a profusely strong way but there was residue of a longing that was evident. I did pick up on that longing and was automatically enveloped into a place inside myself, with thoughts that would consist of what I could do to help.

Just a little back ground about myself, if you will allow. I am naturally inclined to help when I see a need. However, little did I know that this need that I beheld would be one that was not like any need I was used to fixing and being able to proudly say "Finished!" Yes, this need would suck me in like a black hole. This desire that I had to try and help, would be the one that would lead me to the guillotine like Marie Antoinette. This need that I had discerned would never be a quick fixer upper. It would keep me awake at night pondering over in the afternoon, and constantly contemplating on a consistent basis, what I could do to make life easier for you.

Little did I know, it was a trap. I was being set up. Willingly, I choose to be pulled inside of this world of let me make things a little sweeter and nicer for you and to my amazement, I would find that life for me would never be the same again. My life of control and organization, safety and security, would eventually be a life of disorganized beauty and grace, chaos, and intensely climatic thoughts of you that would permeate my mind and be interwoven into every fiber of my being, to the point that if I was to try and get away from it, it would be like pulling the thread out of my favorite cashmere sweater. I had to submit wholeheartedly and without restraint to the fact that I was the one who was in need and in my need to help you, I would be the one who would soon find I was in much need of help.

How on earth could you help me or change my life in any capacity? For starters, will you just be nice? All day, every week and forever, its mere pleasure that I seek. You be the sugar, I'll be the spice. Touch me there, oh yes, that's nice. Here two souls are intertwined, we're making magic happen at the drop of a dime. Here it is, come and get it, take all you need. Take it all, every drop, until I can barely breathe. I bite my lip and clench my fist, you knew exactly what to do and just what I like. I'm a little tired. Let's get some rest.

Peaches & Cream, Strawberries & Chocolate

I am tantalizingly sweet and oh so very delicious,
open your mouth and take a bite of this edible
goodness.
You will be amused as this dessert, once gazed upon,
is consumed.
Just sit back, relax, open wide and swallow;
you'll be glad you did, and watch happiness follow.

Chapter 3

Yummy dessert, a culmination of rich, sweet ingredients, delicately combined for the taste buds to enjoy. Someone had to be in love when the thought occurred, how can I convey my love to that special someone that I am inexplicably, unexplainably in love. I truly believe with all my heart and I am on a mission to persuade you likewise, and I'm sure you will agree that was the reason behind this concoction we call dessert.

You can't convince me this is not true. Should you choose to disagree, maybe it's just a little untrue, but nonetheless and all the same the fact remains, so it's true to me. Being convinced of this very notion that we enjoy dessert because it just makes us feel so much better. Hey, who doesn't like something nice, warm, and scrumptious going down their throat?

As I was saying, the emotions that arise after eating this tasty treat have the ability to evoke something quite special on the inside of the soul, that's simply amazing. I don't know about you, but you know what I'm saying is true. It has the ability to create a certain mood, it just has a way of making everything in life feel sweeter.

Go on! I dare you to indulge in something sweet and I guarantee you that bubbling sensation you sense on the inside will eventually manifest itself comparatively to that which comes quite naturally. Whoever decided to add cream to peaches, dip strawberries into silky warm chocolate, or even set fire to bananas was genius, don't you agree? Well then, with that being said and that being my final conclusion, I now rest my case.

Come on and try it! It will set the mood and create a certain ambience that you and that certain someone will take home with you when that dinner date is finished. One last thing before I let you go. I bet you never thought of this, nor did you know. Take note of the fact that at a wedding, the bride is the center attraction right next to the cake, and is it a coincidence that after a fine meal, almost every culture always finishes off with dessert? Why? You might ask. I'll tell you without hesitation. Dessert has been and will always be what we use to draw us in, and make us consciously aware of the fact that there is and will always be that special thing we call love just bubbling over and waiting to come forth.

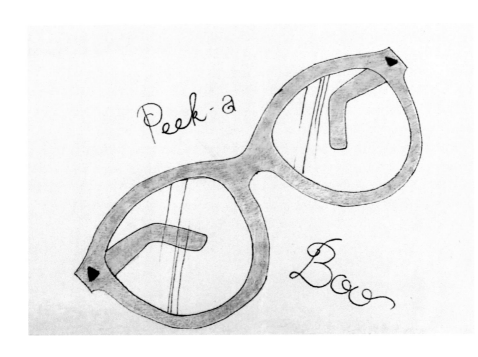

Peek A Boo, do you see me?

Are you still there? Where did you go?
Do you still care? I need to know.
Your body is here, but where's your heart?
When did it leave? When did it start?
Come back to me, I beg and plead.
I miss you so; don't go don't leave!
Peek a Boo, do you see me?
This is not how it's supposed to be.

Chapter 4

He looked up at me with those big brown eyes and it was as if he had looked into and pierced my very soul. There I was standing in front of him, perhaps like how Eve stood in the garden of Eden, clothed only in fig leaves. All and everything about me was revealed and made known to him as he stared at me. I was without garments, I was completely naked and uncovered as he proceeded to stare more intently at me and I loved it, for it excited me immensely.

Everything inside me screamed, "Look harder and longer, and as a matter of fact, don't even blink, because I unashamedly take pleasure and sheer delight in your gaze." I should only hope that as you proceeded to look closer you found that my heart burned for you. Do forgive me for not being a bit more demure and coyishly shy, but at this point your stare and the look in your eyes has all but captivated my mind, body and soul.

Without saying a word, I invite you, my darling, to look upon me as long and in whatever way you like. I welcome it, invite it, and beg it of you. I am now in a place of exasperation and a complete loss of words as I try and gather my feelings. I look for the reasoning behind why I am so smitten and overcome with deliciousness on the inside, as I anticipate the next time I experience the heat and desire that envelopes me when you stare. How you must know that the very thought of the notion that I have in any way shape or form gained an audience by you has caused me great pleasure. Please, I beg, look upon me and come all the more near. Behold me my dear and as often as you will, fill your heart to its contentment and when it is filled, come and look again.

Every time I see you, I wish the seconds, minutes and hours would slow down. I think and almost feel as if someone is playing a cruel trick on me by causing time to speed up, and I get the feeling that perhaps I am in the middle of a chess game, only I am not the one in control of the pieces that are on the board. Tantalizing self-inflicting memories creep into my mind, beyond my control every time we part ways.

I leave, thinking to myself all of the what if's that one could possibly imagine. Small little nonessential things that you do - and have done - invade my mind. Suddenly, I realize that I am head over heels. How I long to tell you and describe all of the uncanny and scrumptious ideas and desires I think about when my mind begins uncontrollably to take me on wild escapades of what it would be like to be close to you. How you feel next to my skin. What it would be like to be so close to you that I can feel your breath as it escapes your nostrils, and ever- so- gently brushes across my face - or better yet, to feel your breath on my neck, ear, lips, and breast.

When I look into your eyes, I see longing, passion, desire and words are not even an option because they fall short and are irrelevant, for they cannot express what the eyes alone can speak. I have at times - and more than I care to mention - looked away because I didn't want you to know and perceive how intensely I desired you. I have wanted you for such a long time. I know without a shadow of a doubt this would be revealed if you were to look at me long enough. So, what do I do? Look away bashfully and look again to make sure you are still watching. You see the eyes – the eyes are an important tool to the one on the receiving end. The eyes reveal the true nature of the heart.

In all actuality, if given the choice, I would prefer to be stared at and not spoken to or approached at all, because without words and by gazing long enough, two people have had an endearing conversation that is and has more worth than a thousand words could speak.

How I love the eyes. The eyes evoke emotion, when words simply fall short. When the heart seems to struggle, trying to retrieve the right words, the eyes will convey that word with a glance. Yes, the eyes attest to the fact that there is something electric that has occurred and has just taken place between us, when words are unnecessary. When you look into my eyes, I come alive and I feel like I want to explode. Look at me, and desire me, please. For in so doing, I just might.

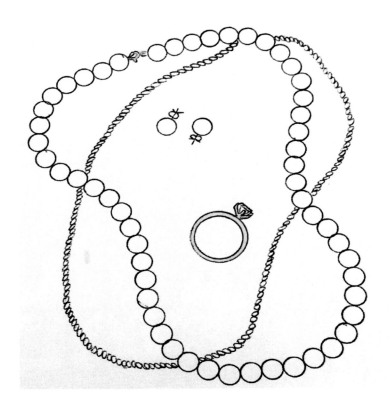

No Thing Compares to You.

To whom or what can I liken you unto?
Nothing or no one can compare.
You're by far my greatest of desires unmatched and
touchable as you are.
There will never be another you, neither near, nor
far,
now I know you're what I've always wanted;
this I knew from the very start.

Chapter 5

When I realized that I had been taken captive by my own free will, heart and emotions similar to that of an innocent lamb; It's going to be okay I convinced myself. I thereby came to the conclusion that if this in fact was my plight, why not accept it. Slowly but swiftly and surprisingly enough it would lead me to a path of no return. I would forever be changed into this person that I myself would no longer be able to recognize because she was in fact unrecognizable.

So, down this path I went reluctantly, but it was in fact by my very own choosing; little did I know, I would never again regain or recover consciousness from the feelings and the emotions that would so freely resurface and exude from on the inside of me to the degree that even as I speak, I am overcome by this overwhelming sensation of passion that I never knew even existed simply because no one in my entire life has ever given me a reason to feel the way that I do right now.

Realizing this I traveled this road nonetheless and it would be a path that I would travel alone. Let me tell you, there is a sort of safety in seclusion that nothing else in the world compares to. I prefer this superficial place of security for which I am always inclined to choose. I have found that it is both stable and secure, poignant yet welcoming.

This place that I now speak of has been a safe haven for me for far too long; that is until you came along. Do you have any idea of just what the very mention of your name does to me on the inside? I will unequivocally tell you: Picture me being ostentatious in my behavior as it pertains to my mannerism. If the opportunity presented itself, I would walk up to you with unrestrained passion, for which I should perhaps feel guilty for feeling no shame at all, for taking hold of you and satisfying myself with such unscrupulous and intense pleasure. At this point, I have immoderately used your body to gratify the unrestrained lasciviousness that lives, moves, and breathes through my body.

Oh yes, I have orchestrated with extreme as well as intense enthusiasm a symphony of songs played by my hands and fingers upon your body. You have reciprocated my actions with a grand song of inaudible noises that perhaps should not be uttered in a public setting. I pity you. If it were in my power, I should like to cause you to forget altogether all the uncanny details of what has just transpired between the both of us.

You see my affections have now taken on a life of there very own. They are now without boundaries. Oh, if you were here right now, I would beg you to not come near me and leave. I am completely out of control emotionally and have gone completely mad - for its unforgivable what has taken place between the two of us.

I have lost myself completely by fulfilling my most ravenous desires, and unmentionable deeds, until you want to get up and walk away but you know that it's not an option. I have stripped you mentally to the point that your unable to even think about what it is that you want or need because all you want to do at this point is please me.

Do you want more? I should like to touch you in places that have never been touched. I want to whisper your name ever so sweetly and in such a way that the sound of my voice reverberates again and again in your ear until it's my voice that you hear, mines and mine alone, repeatedly all throughout the day. I want to cause your imagination to burn and be aroused with ideas on how you will pleasure me until it keeps you awake at night.

I will now refrain from writing any further but there is one more thing you need to know. The words that I have expressed please believe and know that they are true, they come from deep inside my soul because "*No Thing Compares to You.*"

50 Shades of PINK

Chapter 6

Fifty shades of pink

Hot pink, my color of choice if I was going on a hot date with that special someone for the very first time. Where ever a garment could be placed on my body it would be hot pink.

Why, might you say? I thought you'd never ask. Hot pink just makes you feel a certain way. It evokes passion and stimulates emotions and desires that are buried inside, that you can cover up if you were wearing grey or brown. Put on hot pink, and you will unlock this beast that has been dying to come out and play. Go lighter with the color and feel innocent, sweet, and girlie. Go darker and you'll become sensual, irresistible and sexual.

A little history to support my theory. Marilyn Monroe who was known as a sex goddess, was famous for strutting her stuff across the big screen singing *"Diamonds Are a Girl's Best Friend "*with literally every tall, dark, and handsome male wagging their tongue and bowing at her feet, offering her diamonds to choose from as if she were a kid in a candy store. What do you think she was wearing? A hot pink form- fitting mermaid dress with a bow on her bottom as if she was a package waiting to be unwrapped. You think she would have gotten the same attention wearing orange? No. Green? I doubt it. Gray? Absolutely not!

You bored? Need some excitement in your life? Need to spice things up in your bedroom? Go out and get yourself a pink negligee. Want to have that man thinking about you for dessert, before and after that dinner date? Throw on a hot pink fitted dress with hot pink stilettos. Don't forget to accessorize with hot pink polish and lipstick of course. Those dinner plans won't last very long, as you are now that piece of chocolate cake with a cherry on top. It will no longer be you rushing that man to the altar to get married. Talk about turning the tables.

Yes, girl, you put that dress on, go ahead, I dare you. That man will forget that he's got a T-bone steak on his plate. He will more than likely forget why he went to the restaurant altogether. He's got you on his mind. You have now become the object that causes his taste buds to go into maximum overdrive and his mouth to water profusely. Get up and go to the restroom while he is trying to cut his meat and watch him drop his fork because he's too busy trying to look at you. Are you loving the attention?

The power of pink. A million-dollar chain was built off of the name alone- Victoria knew what she was doing with her PINK franchise. Imagine this. It's 8:00 p.m. and you're waiting for your date to pick you up. You haven't seen him in weeks – no, a few months, for whatever reason – when he pulls up there you are standing in something pink. Imagine his thoughts. You can't possibly imagine. Too scrumptious to be repeated. Picture how he looks at you. Hearts are in his pupils, no doubt what his hands are anticipating. Well surely that's imaginable. All because you wore hot pink.

Last but not least, how do you see this date ending? He's thinking "I've got to take her home to meet my mother." You need to prepare for this date ahead of time. Okay, go pick out that wedding dress and the shoes to match and like Marilyn, find the biggest rock that will fit on your finger, because believe me when I tell you that dress did the trick. Bless his little heart.

I know one thing – I'm giving away advice I need to take. I have to go out and buy something pink – HOT pink, that is!

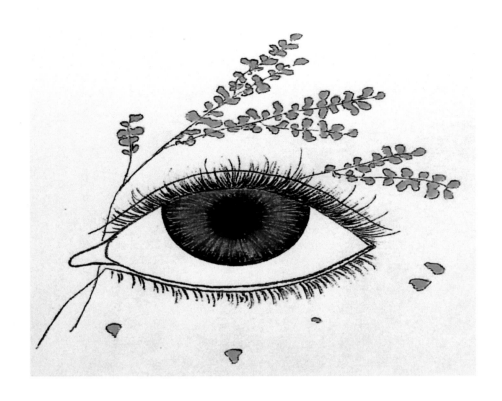

Eyes Closed Wide and Shut

My eyes are closed but I can see.
Imagine you here inside of me.
You come and go throughout the day.
You never leave, you always stay.
I've touched you more than once or twice.
You touched me to and it felt nice.
Were in a room, you closed the door
- you know what's next, we're on the floor.
It was so good. I can't explain;
you hear my voice. I call your name.
These eyes of mine are closed wide and shut;
I dreamed of you, to dream I must.

Chapter 7

As always throughout my day I take the greatest pleasure in conversing with myself. Often, when I do, my thoughts consist of circling swirls of rain water that has meticulously aligned itself into pools, similar to a puddle of water just outside my driveway after a lovely cool spring shower. My imagination, which is quite vivid, you will find, begins to spiral uncontrollably to a place of delight as it's transported to a happy, infinite place of sheer satisfaction and exuberance which entails colors of pink in all shades, materials of lace, and velvet in all forms, and the most billowy and softest cotton your eyes ever did see.

You see, upon meeting you, my love, my darling, everything about me and everything that concerns me causes me to think of you. I now see life from a totally different perspective. I am in a marvelous place of infinite wonder as I have so desperately and hopelessly waited for you to make your feelings for me known on a more obvious level. I am left in bewilderment as I try to understand how I have allowed my heart to be stripped away from me to such a degree, and I fear I shall never retrieve it.

I am very afraid of this place inside me that I now so frequently visit on a continual basis, because it's not a place that I go very often, and truth be told, I have never visited this place in my life at all. This ride has taken me to a place where I cannot even breathe. I feel like the wind has been knocked out of me. You have taken me for the ride of my life, and I am constantly aware of the fact that I will have probably made an imbecile of myself.

But then, who does look well-composed after a ride with such extreme height? I am walking so close to the edge, it would be pure foolishness to not perceive how close I am to falling. Otherwise, I would not think it to be so. Yet I continue on this momentous journey, knowing that it will probably take me down a path that I will never recover from and possibly never, ever again regain consciousness from the same degree that I once knew, before I met you.

I'm falling so fast and so hard, my eyes are no longer able to stay open. They are closed wide and shut. I sincerely and truly believed that I had found the safe, hidden, and secure spot inside my soul, fenced with magical yet deceived contentment, security, and focus. However, it now is, was and has been shattered to all the nothingness that was living inside of me. You must know that my soul and my flesh longs for you and you alone. If you were to just brush up against me, I'm sure it would carry me over for a lifetime, but in all honesty and actuality, that wouldn't be enough. I'd only want more, and it's all because of you.

You're the reason why I can smell, touch, as well as taste color. In my world, you will enjoy shades of the most eloquent pink you ever laid eyes on. You will behold beautiful baby blues that are as cool as the ocean and vibrant hues of lilac that cover every petal on a hydrangea, as a myriad of them so beautifully sweep across an open field, just waiting for one to behold the magnificence of its beauty.

My love, I'm now in a perpetual, hypnotic, and poetic state of graceful color. Will you imagine this world of color to? Its scented with thoughts about you. In my world of color there are no limitations to what you can imagine or conceive. My eyes are closed, yet I see even clearer. Am I now touching parts of your heart that have so desperately longed to be felt and known? I see you completely and I want to uncover you all the more. There are layers of you I want to behold. Will you undress in front of me mentally as well as physically? Will you let me in so that I can see you? Let me stay here for a while. I want to press my face against your chest, inhale, exhale, taking it all in, until I remember the flavor of your scent that I am now covered in.

I am now enjoying you with all five senses and never in my life have I known such extreme gladness. It was indescribable, exhilarating, and magnificently breathtaking. I will say no more. Now close your eyes and close even wider. Now open and shut. Now do it again!

Sticks and Stones May Break My Bones

Why are you so silent? Why do you refuse to speak?
You have denied me air needed to breathe.
Your silence is as cruel as the grave.
It would have been better had you just left
altogether.
However, you decided to stay with your torturing
quietness.
I'd prefer being lost at sea, hoping to be found;
instead I am here, not one year or two but three
and there is nothing left of me.
Quietness is now my companion, unending,
perpetual deadening silence that knows no end.

I am as good as dead, having so many words that were left unsaid.

Chapter 8

Sticks and Stones May Break My Bones

As thoughts of you invade my mind, I rehearse conversations inside my soul that I have had somewhere in another time or place. It does, however, remain to be seen or not if I will ever be graced with the opportunity to have these conversations with you at all. It is unfortunate nonetheless, for the human heart to withhold so many awe-inspiring, free-flowing and precisely imagined words conceived by the human mind to never be mentioned and for the ear to ever be allowed to hear. Words that come from the human heart should be shared amongst individuals to convey their deepest and innermost feelings. There is simply nothing like being able to express your feelings to someone who values what it is that you have to say and even still, the fact remains that after having said everything it is that you believed, you wanted to say you walk away still wanting to say more.

Will you share with me the matters concerning your heart? I want to know the manner in which you feel. Please say to me those things that I so long to hear, that my feelings and emotions are not starved by you. Tell me all the thoughts that you think from dusk till day, so that I will know your true intent. You simply must share your heart with me and bare your very soul, for in so doing, you have helped my broken heart to heal.

You see words are a weapon but it's when you choose not to use any words at all that can possibly do just as much damage. It's when I am left wondering what you think about me, or even if you think about me at all. I'd rather be told that I really don't matter - at least my mind wouldn't be left wondering. Silence, dead, killing me softly, silence will break the spirt and soul just like harsh words. It's in the silence that dreams die, relationships are abandoned and people lose hope. So, please and I beg you don't torture me with silence. It's as cruel as the grave and darker then the night. This silence I speak of is dreadful, horrid, horrendous and plain mean. So, whatever you do please don't let your weapon of choice be silence. I have spent far too many years of my life living in silence. I desire now to only spend the rest of my life surrounded by loved ones who will speak winsome words of love softly in my ears. I plead with you my love to speak, say, and do tell me all that's in your heart. I beg you even more to never stop!

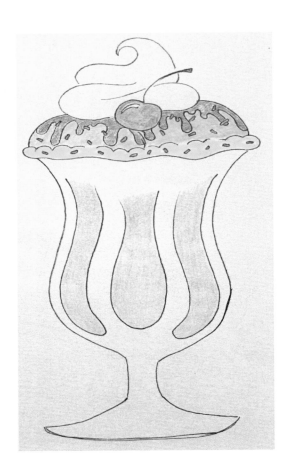

I Love You, I Could Eat You Up!
I am beside myself, for I am immensely, infatuated with you.
I'm smitten and engrossed, having desires and cravings
that are intended for you and only you.
You're the reason for this fire!
Come Now to help put out this flame!
COME!! Put it out again and again and again!

Chapter 9

You have interrupted my world of stability and I now want you in it! Will you go with me on this journey of love and pleasantry that neither you nor I have ever known? Let's take this trip just you and me, away from prying eyes. I am here alone with you and I'm no longer able to hide my feelings and intentions, which are dying to be expressed towards you. I have wanted you so bad for so long that this thirsty, desperate soul of mine weeps agonizingly to be quenched. I do hope you can see through this quiet disposition and demeanor, for right now my only concern is to fulfill these cravings and this unyielding burning passion, by submitting to my inclinations and desires towards you. I anxiously and patiently wait for the day when I can express all the fleshly, appetite-driven and unmentionable deeds I have imagined upon your body, to the degree that I have pleased and gratified my flesh until I only end up wanting you unjustifiably – without restraint, even more.

Imagine mirrors – three or four, plastered on the ceiling, walls and the door. You say what for? If you will wait I will tell you more. They are for our eyes to behold our love and rehearse it over again and again. We're in a room and you lead me to the bed – you stare very deep into the eyes of my soul. I look away bashfully and my lips begin to quiver. You sit me down, I'm on your lap and for a moment, I imagine sitting on the lap of my father because I feel so safe and secure. That thought, however, does not last long because you have turned into my most ardent lover.

Gently, you take my hands as I stand in front of you, while you are sitting on the edge of the bed. You unbutton my blouse from bottom to top and the entire time, your eyes are fixed on mine. My blouse is now on the floor as you have unsnapped my bra and pulled my body into your face. As seconds turn into minutes, my heart is pounding and the delicate part of me throbs uncontrollably. You are ever so gentle and every fiber of my being begins to shake. You reassure me with calm and ease as you look into my eyes, for you know my needs completely. You give me a little smile, but there is no need for us to exchange words.

Suddenly, time has escaped us and we are completely undressed. I am on top of you and you down below. Your mouth and your lips are a perfect fit as you blow on my breast and lick in a circular motion. My mind has already been blown and this isn't even the main course. While I wonder to myself, can I even handle any more? Effortlessly, you gently roll over on top of me and we are now one, and the air that we breathe is as if it came from one body and soul. Anxious excitement bounces off the walls while we are engrossed in rapturous passion, while you proceed to do this and that and I moan like a kitty cat. I like your friend a lot, and even though we have just met, seemingly it's as though we have already been acquainted. He knows every crack, crevice, and corner and I get the feeling that we will be getting to know one another even more in the future.

As our bodies thrust, you can now feel the rush as I am now just being very, very still. I am taking great delight in the scent and taste of your flesh. Now you catch a second wind, and we're at it again, while you sweat profusely as I look up at you. I'm overjoyed that I feel so delicious to you, and that you are working with such vigor, causing your masculinity to be put on display. I love to watch you – just looking at you as you hover over me causes me to be even more aroused. You have no idea what you have done to me. Are you ready for this person that you have created? I'm a monster like Frankenstein's – or worse yet, a King Kong!

You just got up to get a drink of water and as you try to walk out the door, you look back at me, but you can tell I still want more, as stimulating pulses of excitement go all through my body, you come back into the room and we're now on the floor. This is my favorite place of them all. You're a beast and a holy terror, just as I imagined you would be. You blow on my little flame to give me a little air. For so many years it was dry, but now it is flooding.

I say to you, "Come on, let's get up and go sit in that chair." You come in from the back side and we're at it again as I sing melodies of rhapsodic high-squealing pitches that you have joined me in, with an utterance that we probably would not be able to repeat, even if we tried.

It's quiet now, the party is over, and we are just in one another's arms. No, words, just thoughts about how the night went. That's all for now – this chapter is over. I bet you thought it would never end. I know it was rather abrupt, but this guy that I speak of is not even my friend. This is my what if things could perhaps be – I'm sorry to say that it probably wouldn't be me. So, take a big bite, digest this phrase, and swallow. I Love You, I Could Eat You UP! Maybe I'll get the chance tomorrow!

There You Go & Went, Your Gone!

We began as friends but our story would end.
It was over long before it ever started.
I found comfort in sadness, sorrow knew me by name
and more then I want to remember I'd make love to
loneliness.
As strange as this may seem, love for you still remains
and there is no hate or regret.
Although this is the end, my story now begins.
I will never, ever do things this way ever again.

Chapter 10

There you go, twenty years ago when I first laid eyes on you, how very kind you were. You were the friend that I had looked for and was waiting on my entire life, but I wouldn't value or appreciate that precious, priceless gift until it was much too late. I would look for the man I once knew but he was no longer there; his body was but not his heart because he gave it away a long time ago. I would beg and plead, nag and cry for this heart of yours to return to me, but it took an extended trip somewhere and little did I know, it would never return at all.

I would cook and clean, have more children, and get job after job only to come to the realization that none of it would work or bring you back to me. Slowly and surely, the cards would stop coming on special occasions and on days that meant so much to me. All I had left and looked forward too was a simple hello or goodbye - sad to say, I wouldn't get any of that either. You were gone, you left and in your own little way you tried to tell me with the deadening of silence.

I wouldn't accept it, simply because I didn't want to see it. The writing was on the wall. So many years I would wait, hoping, wishing, waiting and praying for the man that I once knew to return. It would take seventeen years for me to realize that you were gone and that you would never return because I never had you. You belonged to everyone but me. I never captivated your heart. A woman knows when the heart of her husband belongs to her, that heart of yours was never mine.

The tears I would cry for so many years, the nights I would sleep alone next to an ice-cold corpse, just a shell of a man whose heart was in his hand held tight for safe keeping. How hard this is to write because the tears even now I still fight. It's been seventeen years of sadness and pain. I can vaguely remember having joy during the day, only the storms in the night. I was lonely, sadness was my middle name. I was surrounded by children, clothes and a famous name.

Just a kind word, anything would have meant so much maybe even a smile or just the slightest hug or touch. The man that I once knew left and walked out a long time ago, and I was replaced and no longer even a friend. Why didn't I even know? These last three years would be the hardest of all, finally realizing that death had won and it was over and we were done! You're the one that threw in the towel; what in the world was I waiting for? I couldn't stop you from walking out that door. So now I pick myself up, dust myself off and except that this is over. Reality has set in and no one is to blame. This is how our story ends, you go your way and I'll go mine. Life will continue on. No need for tears - we'll be just fine.

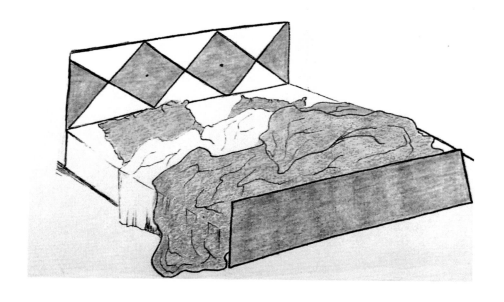

Will You Still Love me in The Morning?

I'm a river, a stream of love that's never ending, ever flowing; pure and true.

A reservoir of temptuous pleasure deep inside.

Tickle your fancy I long to do, and I'll make all your dreams come true; I am yours, you are mine, just wait and see.

Whisper your name I'll gently do, and you'll call mine as I love you.

I've thought this through! Come Hurry Up! Let's Go and Do!

Chapter 11

I write today because I am in fear of the unknown, but allow me to be very intentional in expressing my feelings and bear with me as I try and tell you why. My feelings for you are like streams of water going in only one direction and they lead to only one result: I must have you! I am enraged by strong urges and wantonness to the degree that perhaps by your standards, you would think me to be a loose and immoral woman.

Who am I? I can hardly even recognize myself! Look at what you have done to me! I am your slave, I am your toy and you have my permission to do whatever you can think or imagine. All day long I am filled with intense, climatic, quintessential thoughts about you. I want to be your hostage of erotic fantasies which have been contrived and tucked away deep inside your heart and soul. Make me and mold me into the vessel that you, my captor, desire me to be. Whatever you ask me, I will do, for it's my intention to please you, for your wish is my command. As of right now neither of us waste any time, we don't dare lie down, we stand. You are now lost inside of the soft and sensual delicateness of my body. You started off gently but now you have switched gears and now you're in maximum overdrive and I, yes, I myself am about to lose my mind.

As we have shared one another for the first time, this one question permeates deep inside my heart. My soul is buried in agony and torment just thinking about it. Did I please you? Was I able to fulfill all of your desires? The very thought of this makes me want to run and hide. I ponder this daily, for it has been a perpetual feast of fear all day long. I can no longer delay this question, that do-or-die, thought-provoking question that rings loud and true. This question that is so tenably rehearsed in my inner ear that I coerce deep inside, over and over again. It keeps me awake at night, as well as haunts me during the day. That million-dollar question: that if I give you me, will you stay?

If I could, I would turn back time, merge the past and the present, to make life simpler. How, you might ask? I would change my very footsteps and we never would have met. I'd rearrange every minute and every hour and I would not have come a moment sooner – if it were up to me, perhaps much later. You see, after all the excitement has passed, it's the morning after, will you regret the past? I see you and want you still, but fear you walking out the door. Will You Still Love Me in The Morning? That fear has gripped me once more.

NOTES

Conclusion: Our Happily Ever After

I write this final chapter for all of you who, like me, in spite of all the heartbreak, disappointment, and pain refuse to give up on believing that there is a happily ever after. There has to be. The simple fact that you decided to pick up this book and you are now reading it proves that your still very hopeful. If you have been fortunate enough to have found yours, pay it forward and pass this book to someone else who may have lost hope. For the rest of you, your dream come true is closer than you might think!

While waiting to be found by him or her, try working on you. Give that person something special once you have been found. Don't get impatient and feel like you are running out of time. If you have been given more time, that just means your worth the wait. You need to know that you are a gift, a package so to speak, and it will take a lifetime to unveil the secret treasure concealed and locked away in your heart. Yes, the matters of your heart are much to be compared to a pearl of great price, that has to be sought after, before being beautifully adorned and worn around the neck of an individual.

Know your worth and value, and others will treat you accordingly. You are a priceless gift, containing ideas and expressions worthy of sharing with someone who will appreciate and value your worth. If you have yet to be found, just look on the bright side - all that means is that you are being graced with more time to work on you and present to someone special your very best you. Enjoy the time you have, find out who you are. Get to know you, like you and laugh at you. There is someone special evolving into someone all the more wonderful every day.

Life is magical, marvelous and magnificent. It awaits with anticipation to unfold before your very eyes, but you must wait on it. Hope with expectancy and it will come. I promise you, your happily ever after is silently knocking at the door of your heart. Be still, listen, and be ready to let love in. Do you hear it? Don't go chasing after it, allow it to find you. Love is all around - I'm telling you, my friend, if you will only believe and never stop believing in the gift and the power of love.

You cannot possibly fathom how anxious love is, and has waited to find you at the right place at the right time. That is the magic question: are you in in the right place at the right time? Try and consider it, if you will, that love has been traveling for centuries, defying the very existence of time and space, just to meet you during this particular time in your life. Love has a mind of its very own and the very fact that you are still engaged and reading proves that love is on the very inside of you as well.

Hope Again! Dream Again! More than anything else learn to love you again. Love you because you deserve that! You can't give something away that you don't have. Find out who you are and just do you! Next thing you know, before you realize, love has laid eyes on you, and you have been hit by Cupid's arrow.

Journal

Journal

Journal

Journal

Journal

Made in the USA
Lexington, KY
06 January 2018